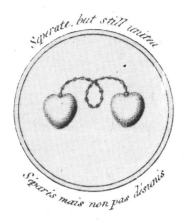

Seperate, but still united

Séparés mais non pas désunis

Consacré à l'Amour

To Immortality

A l'Immortalité.

I comfort

Je console

Be thankful

Sois reconnoissant

I change

Je ne change qu'en mourant

An Introduction to
Sentimental Jewellery

FRONT COVER
See plate 14

FRONT ENDPAPER *(left)*
Plate from F. Knight, *Gems and Device Book,* 1836

FRONT ENDPAPER *(right)*
Plate 52 from F. Knight, *Gems and Device Book,* 1836

1 ▶
Locket
Enamelled gold, the obverse (not
shown) set with diamonds, the
reverse decorated with a crowned
heart pierced by arrows between
the letters C and B, the edge
engraved *fidel . Iusq . a . la . mort . le
. pareil . de . vous . a . mon . confort*
(faithful unto death, the likeness
of you is my comfort)
French, about 1610–20
H. 2.5 cms
Given by Dame Joan Evans, PPSA
M.110-1975

An Introduction to
Sentimental Jewellery

Shirley Bury
Formerly Keeper, Department of Metalwork
Victoria & Albert Museum

LONDON: HER MAJESTY'S STATIONERY OFFICE

Copyright © Shirley Bury 1985
First published 1985

Series editor Julian Berry

Designed by HMSO Graphic Design
Printed in the UK for HMSO

ISBN 0 11 290417 3
Dd 718120   C65

ACKNOWLEDGEMENTS
I am deeply grateful to Her Majesty the Queen for her Gracious permission to quote
from Queen Victoria's Journal; to Miss Jane Langton, MVO, the Royal Archivist,
Mr Jeremy Whitaker for the colour photographs and to my colleagues Harold
Barkley, Françoise B. de B. Crichton, Michael Holmes, Michael Snodin, Anna
Somers Cocks and Jane Stancliffe for advice.
Shirley Bury
March 1984

ORDER OF PLATE CAPTIONS
Where more than one object is illustrated, the sequence of the captions to a plate is
clockwise, starting from the top.

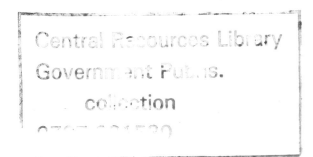

HER MAJESTY'S STATIONERY OFFICE

Government Bookshops

49 High Holborn, London, WC1V 6HB
13a Castle Street, Edinburgh EH2 3AR
9-21 Princess Street, Manchester M60 8AS
Southey House, Wine Street, Bristol BS1 2BQ
258 Broad Street, Birmingham B1 2HE
80 Chichester Street, Belfast BT1 4JY

Government Publications are also available through booksellers

The full range of Museum publications is displayed and sold at the
Victoria & Albert Museum, South Kensington, London SW7 2RL

Introduction

Sentimental jewellery has always been valued as a tangible expression of emotion. To many people it is still almost as inconceivable that a woman should engage herself to be married without receiving a ring as it is for her to go through the marriage ceremony without receiving another.

But sentimental jewellery is occasioned by a much wider range of feelings and conditions than those relating to betrothal and marriage. Affection for family and friends, the passion of lovers, loyalty to a monarch or a cause, religious devotion and the death of loved ones have all been commemorated by jewels; the tokens of dalliance being an especially fruitful field. In Congreve's play, 'Love for Love' (1695), Tattle offers as proof of his numerous conquests 'letters, lockets, pictures and rings', well aware that these would clinch the matter with his hearers.[1]

The jewels illustrated and discussed here are all sentimental jewels of one kind or another; they comprise many types of personal ornament but exclude rings, which are the subject of a companion book in this series.[2] Ranging in date from the seventeenth to the nineteenth century, when the genre was in a particularly flourishing state, they include pieces specially commissioned by rich and fashionable clients and others produced from standardised components for the popular market.

These works frequently have in common certain decorative motifs such as hearts, an obvious sentimental device whose meaning has nevertheless to be read according to the purpose of the jewel. If the object of love was alive, the heart signified betrothal, marriage [plate 11b] or a gesture of love and friendship [plate 31a]; if dead, grief for the departed [plate 2a]. Cupids, another popular motif, represent the triumph of love on the one hand [plate 2c] and personify the angels on the other [plate 3d]: these opposing uses stem from complementary traditions of secular and religious symbolism which are outlined below.

Emblems, Devices and Hieroglyphics

Symbols, which to the initiated represented many layers of meaning, preoccupied the writers, artists and craftsmen of the Renaissance. As they were drawn from the general pool of classical and medieval learning, they were largely literary in origin; the visual application followed. The abstract emblem, a complex symbol which even in visual form frequently required a literary interpretation to be fully understood, has been particularly esteemed for this reason by the learned. The idea of the emblem, conceived by an Italian nobleman in the 1520s, was taken up at his suggestion by two celebrated lawyers. One, Andrea Alciati (1492-1550), produced a series of verses on the lines of Greek and Latin epigrams. These were published by Heinrich Steyner at Augsburg in 1531 under the title *Emblemata;* each emblem composed of an epigram, an allegorical illustration and a motto, all reciprocally interpreting each other.

Alciati, who was we suspect principally concerned with his poems, realised even before the book appeared that the emblems, translated into visual form, might be of use to craftsmen; his belief was to be confirmed. One of his emblems, that of the serpent biting its own tail, signifying eternity, was still in use in the nineteenth century [plates 5b and 7b]. The success of Alciati's book prompted a host of imitative publications all over Europe. In England, Geoffrey Whitney produced his *Choice of Emblems* in 1586.

The device, older than the emblem, originated (as the *devise*) in the chivalric culture of France in the fourteenth century. Usually signifying a personal preoccupation or quality, it furnished material for heraldic crests. Later, in Italy, where it was taken up with enthusiasm, the device (Italian, *impresa*) received much the same literary treatment as the emblem, though the first Italian book to be devoted to devices (Paolo Giovio's *Dialogo dell' Imprese*) was published without illustrations in 1555. An illustrated version of the work was brought out in France four year later.[3] Though it was held that only those of royal, noble or knightly rank had the right to bear devices, some of the imagery passed into general artistic currency. It must be admitted that many devices to do so were fairly obvious, including the constancy of the turtle-dove [back endpaper and 13a] and the inviolate quality of

2
Three 17th-century English lockets

a
Heart-shaped, silver, commemorating Charles I
(1600-49).
The reverse (shown) inscribed *I live and dy in loyalty*
above a heart pierced with arrows; inside, a medallion
of the King and other inscriptions
*c.*1650
H. 2.3 cms
Croft Lyons Bequest M.811-1926

b
Copper-gilt, containing a miniature of Major Williams
Carlos (d. 1689) — shown in two parts
The reverse *(right)* engraved with Charles II and Carlos
hiding in an oak tree at Boscobel House after the battle

of Worcester in 1651, and the obverse *(left)* with the
Carlos arms.
(Charles II, crowned at Scone, marched southwards
with his followers in 1651 but was routed by Cromwell's
army at the battle of Worcester. Eluding his pursuers,
he eventually escaped to France)
c. 1660
H. 5.4 cms
898-1904

c
Heart-shaped, silver, with an embossed Cupid. Maker's
mark RA. The border inscribed *Noe heart more true then
(sic) mine to you*
2nd half of the 17th century
H. 2.5 cms
Johnson Bequest M.3-1958

the diamond. The miniature of about 1600 by Isaac Oliver in plate 6 is in effect a portrait incorporating a device. The wistful young man fingers a locket which apparently contains a picture of his beloved, as he is portrayed against the flames of love. This device may have had its origins in the imagery of the Italian poet Petrarch,[4] but it could equally be an allegory of the lover either as the legendary salamander feeding on the flames, or engulfed by the fires of the torch of love itself.[5] The charm of such symbols is that a single interpretation is impossible.

Many compilations drew on the *Hieroglyphics* (of the enigmatic character) by Horapollo, an Egyptian who wrote his work in or about the fourth century AD. His manuscript, known only by a Greek translation which was acquired in 1419 and taken to Florence, was copied, pored over, printed in Greek in 1505 and in a Latin translation a decade later. New translations and editions were produced throughout the century, some of the later versions carrying illustrations. Horapollo, who apparently possessed only an imperfect knowledge of ancient Egyptian hieroglyphs, followed the Greek custom of regarding them as allegories concealing the occult wisdom of the Egyptian priest-hood. The idea found favour in the sixteenth century, and hieroglyphs were widely held to be the true forerunners of devices and emblems.

The vogue for emblem and device books, rapidly spreading through many European countries, encouraged the pursuit of further novelties, even in Italy, and such disparate sources as astrology and classical coins were ransacked for material.

In the early years of the seventeenth century, when intellectural interest was still high, a new vogue for motifs taken from the classical poets was started. The God of Love, Cupid, plays and suffers through the early seventeenth century works of Daniel Heins (Heinsius), whose *Emblemata Amatoria* appeared in 1610 (see frontispiece), and Otto Van Veen (Vaenius) who drew on Ovid for his *Amorvm Emblemata: Emblemes of Loue with Verses in Latin, English, and Italian* two years earlier.[6] The title page of a French version of Van Veen's book *(Emblèmes d'Amour)* is embellished with an amatory trophy, comprising a bow, quiver and torch bound with a true-lover's knot. Such motifs found their way into the applied arts. The Cupid embossed on the front of one of the two mid-seventeenth century heart-shaped lockets in plate 2c has drawn his bow so that the arrow is positioned eternally for flight, with the usual message underlined by the inscription: *NOE HEART MORE TRUE THEN (sic) MINE TO YOU.* By the second half of the century, however, the stream of inspiration was beginning to run dry, and subsequent publications added little to the existing popular repertory of symbols which by degrees lost some of their finer shades of meaning.

The second heart-shaped piece [plate 2a] commemorates the execution of Charles I. The back, which is illustrated, is inscribed: *I live and Dy in Loyalty* and engraved with a heart penetrated by arrows. Numerous small lockets were produced in homage to the King both before and after his death. Most were small enough to be worn by his supporters unnoticed under their shirts, an important consideration during the Civil Wars and the Protectorate. The hazards overcome by the royalists are exemplified by a large copper-gilt locket [plate 2b] which depicts Major William Carlos and Charles II concealed in an oak tree at Boscobel to avoid detection by the Parliamentary forces after the Battle of Worcester in 1651. Inside the locket is a miniature of Carlos and a verse more remarkable as an expression of loyalty than its poetic qualities.[7]

The popularity of Cupid and other devices of love such as true-lover's knots and hearts did not prevent their assuming another existence as religious emblems during the Counter-Reformation; a development of widespread importance in Catholic countries, which is apparent in such publications as Van Veen's *Amoris Divini Emblemata* (1615). The success of the transformation is demonstrated by the enamelled gold locket of about 1675 in plate 4a; acquired by the V&A in 1870 from the treasury of the Cathedral of the Virgin of the Pillar in Saragossa, Spain, its fashionable decoration is an elaborate religious iconography which includes two symbols borrowed from the repertory of amatory devices. Below the triangle at the top, symbolising the Trinity, is a bow against a true-lover's knot which here signifies devotion. Four of the drops are suspended from esclavos (s with a line through = clavo, *ie* slave); a punning symbol which had an amatory as well as a devotional application. The figure of a Fate spinning the thread of destiny on the locket in plate 4b is among the allegorical personifications fashionable from about the mid-sixteenth century. Cesare Ripa's *Iconologia,* first published in an unillustrated edition at Rome in 1593, remained a prime source of inspiration for these figures for almost two hundred years.

New versions of the old emblem and device books published in the eighteenth and nineteenth centuries showed a marked tendency to revert to the old secular interpretation of Cupid as the symbol of earthly love, ignoring or diminishing his spiritual aspects. Cupid as cherub was left to the hair workers' productions which will be discussed presently. Samuel Fletcher, a seal engraver working in London, was one of many who concentrated on Cupid in his *Emblematical Devices* (1810), though he also drew on a wide range of traditional motifs, illustrating them with mottos in both English and French. Fletcher was followed (and copied) by Knight's *Gems and Device Book* (1836). As the titles indicate, the books were mainly aimed at the expanding market for fancy seals, for in late Georgian England letters were still fastened with hot sealing-wax on which the engraved device of the writer was impressed. But they had a wider application, as is shown by some of the designs in Knight's work (see front end papers). The happy image of the insect settling on a rose (I *settle* or *Je me fixe*) shows parallel symbolism to the sorrowful enamelled gold locket of about 1810 in plate 5b which depicts the flower withering and a butterfly, robbed of its nectar, flying off. The butterfly (emblem of the

Four English mourning slides
In enamelled gold and gold wire on hair, set in gold frames under faceted crystal. The slides are fitted with loops on the back, through which ribbon was threaded for wear

a
A standing skeleton holding an arrow and an hour-glass, flanked by the initials IC. The reverse engraved: *IC obt 6 jul aeta 3 ye 8 mo* (IC died 6 July aged 3 years 8 months)
c. 1700
L. 2.3 cms
M.11-1960

b
A skull on a winged hour-glass and two cherubs with trumpets on an enamelled coffin, inscribed *MEM. MORI* and with the initials *EB*. The reverse engraved: *obt 6 Feb 1697*
1697
L. 2 cms
M.12-1960

c
Slide converted into a brooch; two angels bearing a celestial arrow and a cypher. The reverse engraved: *Sr. An: Leake Kil'd by ye French off of Malaga Augt 13th 1704*
18th century
L. 2 cms
Given by Dame Joan Evans, PPSA
M.124-1962

d
A recumbent skeleton on a coffin inscribed: *I REST,* and two angels bearing a cartouche with the initials *MT*
c. 1700
L. 2 cms
M. 14-1960
a, b, d, Frank Ward Bequest

soul in Neoclassical art), taken together with the ground of plaited hair and inscriptions expressive of sorrow, point to it being a mourning jewel, though the name or initials of the deceased are lacking. The pendant is encircled by the traditional serpent of eternity.

Fletcher's plates include a series of idiosyncratic scripts, ranging from so-called Etruscan and Egyptian to Norman and Gothic. These were used for love inscriptions on rings, pendants and seals which could only be interpreted by those possessing the key to the alphabets. Knight's book even incorporated a few plates of rebuses under the title 'hieroglyphics', which were likewise aimed at the mass market for sentimental devices. 'I expect a line in return' is rendered as an eye, the letter x and the word RETURN with a line through it; 'Use me well' as two yew-trees, the word ME and a well. Puzzles such as these, having served their turn on cast paste seals and similar items of cheap jewellery, have survived to entertain children in newspapers and magazines.

4

Two 17th-century enamelled lockets

a

Gold, set with table-cut diamonds and hung with seven pendants; the triangle at the top symbolises the Trinity, the fashionable bow below it is silhouetted against a true-lover's knot and four pendants are supported by esclavos, a common punning symbol of devotion
From the Treasury of the Cathedral of the Virgin of the Pillar, Saragossa
French or Spanish, c. 1675
L. 6 cms
326-1870

b

Silver-gilt (reverse shown); a figure of Fate spinning our Destiny, inscribed *L'Amour s'exerce*
French, 2nd half of the 17th century
H. 4.7 cms
1310-1871

5

Two early 19th-century English lockets in enamelled gold

a

Frame inscribed *LOUISA . BOHUN . OB . 14 . APR . 1816 . AET . 18*, enclosing a miniature of a girl in Elizabethan costume. The reverse inscribed *Frances . Bohun . Ob . 1 . Aug : Aet : 15*
H. 3.9 cms
M.117-1962

b

Frame edged with the serpent of eternity, enclosing a drooping rose bush and a butterfly in enamelled gold on a background of hair; inscribed *LA . ROSE . FLETRIE . LE . PAPILLON . S'ENVOLE* (the rose withers, the butterfly flies away) and *NAPPED . IT . FELL . TO . THE . GROUND*. The reverse inscribed *And such I exclaim'd is the pitiless part, Some art by the delicate Mind, Regardless of Wringing and Breaking a Heart, already to sorrow resigned*
c. 1810
H. 4.8 cms
M.123-1962
a and b given by Dame Joan Evans, PPSA

6

6
Miniature of an unknown man
Pigment in gum arabic on vellum,
mounted on a playing card
Isaac Oliver (*c.* 1560-1617)
c. 1600
H. 6.6 cms
P. 5-1917

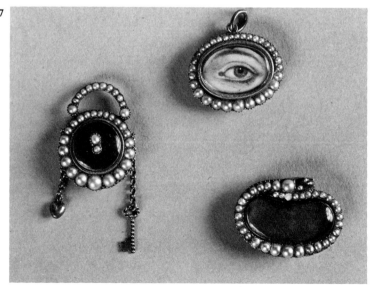

7

7
Three English jewels in gold with
seed pearl borders, *c.* 1800-10

a
Eye locket, the frame enclosing a
miniature of an eye painted on
ivory. The reverse with hair and
pearls
L. 2.5 cms
935-1888

b
Brooch with serpent frame with a
ruby eye, enclosing a glass-fronted
locket for hair
L. 2.8 cms
957-1888

c
Pendant in the form of a padlock,
with pendent key and heart. The
glass centre also set with pearls
L. 2 cms
Given by Dame Joan Evans, PPSA
928-1888

8
Oil
Margaret Hallyday, wife of Sir Edward Hungerford
Cornelius Johnson
1631
Ranger's House, Blackheath

9
A chatelaine and an etui, both
English

a
Chatelaine in pinchbeck and gilt
copper set with agate, hung with a
seal and an egg-shaped container
for a thimble, the rim inscribed on
enamel *JE NE M'ATTACHE
QU'A VOUS* (I only belong to
you)
Mid 18th century
H. 13.5 cms
Given by Dame Joan Evans, PPSA
M.269-1975

b
Etui, agate mounted in gold,
set with an emerald and three
brilliant-cut diamonds. The
underside engraved *Masham from
her Lovin Dux*. A gift from Queen
Anne to Mrs. Masham
c. 1712
H. 9 cms
Jones collection 950-1882

9

Love and Mourning Jewellery

It is scarcely surprising that, with their common origin in emblem and device books, the souvenirs of living loves and dead ones have frequently looked alike, a phenomenon that has already been noted. Only close inspection of the symbols, sometimes aided by inscriptions, distinguishes the role of Cupids as amatory or religious in intent. One such device (crowned in this instance to indicate the status of its owner) embellishes the back of an early-seventeenth-century French miniature case in plate 1. The initials of the lovers, C and B, flank the

10
Design for a jewel; pen and wash
Italian (Florentine), mid 18th
century
P & D 7908.64

heart, and round the edge of the locket an inscription is engraved: *Fidel. iusq.-a.-la.-mort. le pareil. de. vous. a. mon. confort.* (Faithful unto death, the likeness of you is my comfort), an ambiguous inscription which alludes to the picture once contained in the case. The nearest visual equivalent to this assertion is Isaac Oliver's amorous young man [plate 6] who, himself a picture, fingers a miniature case containing the portrait of his love. But is the French piece a mourning jewel, or does the inscription merely refer to the reassurance derived from the miniature when the beloved one is away from home? The brightness of the enamel colours indicates that the loved one was in fact alive.

The mid-seventeenth-century French locket in plate 4b presents no problems of identification. The front (not shown) is decorated in painted enamel with a man and a woman in classical costume clasping hands before a flaming altar, with the accompanying inscription, *Mon Coeur s'adresse* (My heart is dedicated). The classical female figure on the reverse, carrying a distaff, personifies the Fate that weaves our destiny. That the destiny is love in this instance is signified by the motto, *L'Amour s'exerce,* perhaps best rendered in English as 'Love renews itself'. The piece must have been a betrothal or marriage gift.

The devices of love often infiltrated themselves into expensive stone-set jewellery. Suspended below the central crowned motif of the diamond necklace worn by Margaret Hallyday in her portrait of 1631 is a small heart with its own three pendants [plate 8]. The daughter of an alderman and Lord Mayor of London, Margaret Hallyday married Sir Edward Hungerford (1596-1648) and the necklace was probably part of the marriage jewellery given her by her husband, who was afterwards active in the Parliamentary cause in the Civil War.

The splendid baroque jewellery worn by the Court beauties of the late seventeenth century was, however, only occasionally depicted in detail in their portraits, which create an overriding impression of large diamonds and pearls threaded through the hair, suspended from the ears, looped around throats, trailing across shoulders and falling to waists. Nevertheless some love motifs were incorporated in grand baroque designs of the most formal type. An engraved design of 1663 by Gilles Légaré for a sévigné (a bow-shaped ornament, usually worn on the bodice) is reproduced in Joan Evans, *A History of Jewellery* 1100-1870.[8] From the bow hang two seals, one of which has a heart as its apex. The modest little mourning slide in plate 24b, commemorating Queen Mary II of England (1662-94), shows that not all baroque jewellery was ambitious and expensive. Probably mass-produced as a speculation by an enterprising jeweller anxious to capitalize on the Queen's death, it lacks the hair that would be expected of a piece commissioned by her husband, William III. Moreover the centre is stamped from a single piece of foil.[8]

Sentimental messages from friend to friend were always popular. An early-eighteenth-century agate etui (a case for implements such as tweezers, scissors, toothpicks and the like) [plate 9b] is evidence of a friendship of a rather grand nature. The piece is inscribed on the base:

Masham from her Lovin Dux. This cryptic message can be deciphered; the donor, 'Dux' (latin Leader) was Queen Anne (1665-1714) and the recipient Mrs Masham, who had supplanted the imperious Duchess of Marlborough in the affections of her sovereign in 1711. Mrs Masham must have been triumphant as she wore the etui (suspended from the waist), for its utility was as nothing compared with its larger meaning. Unlike the Duchess who had introduced her into the Queen's Household, Mrs Masham inclined to the Jacobite cause, though Anne died without being persuaded to confirm the Old Pretender as her successor.[9]

In the 1730s, as the baroque began to give way to the light-hearted asymmetric rococo manner, sentimental devices assumed a new prominence. The two hearts in the anonymous mid-eighteenth-century Florentine design in plate 10 are covered with lines to indicate the cutting of the stones from which they were to be made; the parasol tipped to one side, reminiscent of those carried by figures in Chinoiserie ornament, gives the piece an Oriental air. In addition to classical symbols like Cupid's bow and arrows and the flaming torches of love, motifs drawn from nature such as turtle doves, traditional symbols of constancy[10] were ingeniously introduced into forms inherited from the baroque including girandole earrings (comprising a top and three, sometimes five) pendants. The back end papers are taken from the *Traité des Pierres Précieuses* of 1762 by Pouget fils (Jean-Henri-Prosper Pouget, a Parisian jeweller who died in 1769). The author claimed in his foreword to the book that the new mode in jewellery had been evolved some thirty years earlier by Augustin Duflos, who carried the style from Paris to the Spanish court at Madrid. But the rococo manner was everywhere, its gaiety exemplified by the left-hand back end-paper which mainly illustrates ornaments for the coiffure or headgear in the form of a series of miniature hats, trimmed with the usual accoutrements of love as well as musical instruments, marine motifs and, of course, flowers and feathers.

Hearts worn on heads and ears, if not on sleeves, were matched by hearts on bodices and throats, wrists and elsewhere, openly testifying to the wearer's appetite for love and affection. The double-sided crystal heart locket in plate 25b, flaunts both its inscription and hair. But an occasional ambiguity remains. The mid-eighteenth-century diamond, ruby and emerald brooch in plate 11a, in the form of a dove carrying a sprig in its beak, is a well-known religious symbol of good tidings, deriving from the return of the dove bearing an olive branch to the Ark: [11] perhaps the bird brooch signified tidings of an amatory nature to its original owner?

An agate and gilt metal chatelaine [plate 9a], roughly contemporary with the dove brooch, was, like Mrs Masham's etui, designed to be suspended from the waist. A watch (now missing) once hung from the centre, but two ancillary pieces are still in place on the sides, one a seal and the other an egg-shaped container of agate caged in metal, a trinket or charm which usually housed a thimble. The container bears the inscription, *JE NE M'ATTACHE QU'À VOUS* (I belong only to you) on an enamelled ground, a twofold allusion to the chatelaine itself and to the wearer. A similar conceit appears on a carved agate scent flask in the shape of a boy holding a lamb as if proffering it to the spectator [plate 12]. Ornamented with diamond sparks and enamelled gold, the boy's collar carries the legend, *JE VOUS L'OFFRE* (I give you this), which may refer to the original gift, to the scent in the flask or even, as a tertiary meaning, to the boy's gesture with the lamb.

11

12

12
Agate scent flask, in the form of a boy holding a lamb. The gold collar set with diamond sparks and enamelled; inscribed *JE VOUS L'OFFRE* (I give you this)
English, *c.* 1760
H. 9.2 cms
Murray Bequest M.1052-1920

11
French jewels set with diamonds

a
Dove brooch, set with brilliant-cut diamonds, emeralds and rubies in silver mounts
c. 1755
L. 5.5 cms
M.56-1962

b
Pair of bracelet clasps in gold, set with brilliant-cut diamonds and blue paste. One bears the cipher of Marie Antoinette, and the other the turtle doves and hymeneal torches used as a device at the time of her marriage to Louis XVI. Both have the wreath of Trianon, symbolising the splendours of the French Crown
c. 1770
H. 5 cms
M.51 and a-1962
a and b given by Dame Joan Evans, PPSA

Two amatory jewels, English or Continental

a

Gold brooch, the frame set with pearls, enclosing a painted ivory plaque representing two doves on a basin of applied gold foil, below the inscription *LAMOUR*
Late 18th century
H. 2.2 cms
970–1888

b

Gold pendant, the frame enclosing a composition under stars of mother-of-pearl on blue paste, depicting two flaming hearts on an altar inscribed *A VOUS DEDIE;* with a basket of flowers nearby
c. 1800
H. 2.8 cms
931–1888

14

Two early-19th-century French jewels

a

Brooch in enamelled gold, set with carnelians, pearls and emeralds
L. 6.4 cms
Given by Dame Joan Evans, PPSA
M.37-1962

b

Eight symbols of the Ages of Man in gold, carnelian and enamel, mounted on a hoop. Paris warranty mark for 1809-19
L. 5.5 cms (approx)
Given by Mrs. A. M. Lees
M.103-g-1945

The spread of Neoclassicism from the 1760s onwards did nothing to abate the popularity of sentimental devices. A pair of diamond and blue paste bracelet clasps of 1770 in plate 11b demonstrate the continuance of the tradition; only the restrained oval shape of the clasps proclaims the new style. The clasps, furnished on the reverse with loops to which strings of stones or pearls were attached to form bracelet bands, were made as souvenirs of the marriage in 1770 of Marie Antoinette (1755-93), the fourth daughter of the powerful Empress Maria Theresa of Austria, with the Dauphin Louis (1754-93), later Louis XVI of France; the bride was only fourteen at the time of her wedding. One clasp is decorated with a trophy of turtle doves, two hymeneal torches (perhaps one is Cupid's quiver), a wreath of Trianon symbolising the splendours of the French crown above, and a forget-me-not below, in diamonds mounted on blue paste within a border of brilliants. The other, in the same materials, bears the Princess's cipher or monogram with a wreath above and a forget-me-knot below. The clasps were probably given by Marie Antoinette to one of her ladies to mark the marriage, launched in brilliance and ended by the guillotine in 1793. The use of vitreous paste in the clasps was a common eighteenth-century practice [see plate 28c]. Cast glass cameos were also widespread; the pendent commemorative brooch set with a paste cameo portrait of John Wesley (1703-91), evangelist and leader of methodism, [plate 28a] was probably produced as a souvenir after his death.

A brooch and a locket in plate 13 exemplify the amatory equivalent of painted sepia mourning jewels which are discussed presently. Such pieces were produced in quantity, and their maxims are generalized, not specific. The brooch, bordered by seed pearls, is set with a painted ivory plaque representing a pair of turtle doves perched on a basin of applied gold foil; the message is underlined by the word L'AMOUR at the top. The locket is set with a composition, executed in mother-of-pearl on paste, of two flaming hearts on an altar inscribed A VOUS DEDIE (dedicated to you); a trail of flowers and a basket filled with sprays are decorative appendages. Such pieces were produced on the Continent, and also in England largely by immigrant craftsmen.

A brooch in the form of a traditional trophy of love, with bow, quiver, arrows and a flaming torch, surmounted by a pair of turtle doves, and with a pendant of two fiery hearts encircled by elegant enamelled gold chains [plate 14a] is probably French and dates to about 1800. Another piece, an elegant trifle to wear on a chain or a chatelaine and made in Paris between 1809 and 1819, comprises eight symbols of the Ages of Man [plate 14b]. The majority correspond with Shakespeare's Seven Ages, enumerated in *As You Like It,* from the cradle of the infant to the spectacles of old age.[12] Not really sentimental (except perhaps as a Memento Mori, literally 'keep death in your thoughts'), the piece is a conceit of the kind popular in what was known as *bijouterie de fantaisie* in France and fancy jewellery in England.

The fashion for medallions (the large round or oval pendants often incorporating lockets) which were worn by every fashionable woman in the late eighteenth century continued, though to a lesser extent, in the first two decades of the new century. They were mainly set with portrait miniatures which more often than not were displayed on the face of the jewels. Such pieces were frequently worn on long chains. Many were tokens of affection; others were mourning jewels. The piece in plate 5a, a mourning locket dated 1816, is smaller than the medallions in vogue before 1800 but is otherwise characteristic of the type. The miniature represents Louisa Bohun in a costume reflecting the rage for Mary, Queen of Scots; an inscription on the reverse records the death of a relative at the age of fifteen.

Several variations were played on the theme of the portrait. Silhouettes (named after Etienne de Silhouette (1709-67), a French author and politician) were popular on the Continent and in England; two examples by one of the leading professional artists in the genre, John Miers (1758-1821), are illustrated in plate 15. Both are set in small brooches which were known at the time as pins and only later in the nineteenth century as lace pins (so-called because they were often used to fasten kerchiefs or lace at the neck). One has a locket fitting at the back. A late eighteenth-century innovation, popular in several countries, was a portrait miniature of an eye of a loved one, which had the additional charm of mystery, for it was tantalisingly difficult to identify the sitter. The miniaturist Richard Cosway (1740-1821) is said (probably erroneously) to have invented the genre;[13] at any rate he painted the right eye of the Prince of Wales (later George IV) for a locket attached to a bracelet intended as a gift to the Prince's morganatic wife Mrs Fitzherbert in 1799.[14] The eye locket in plate 7a, set with hair at the back, was possibly once owned by a man as the sitter is female. Men still wore lockets, sometimes on their watch fobs, sometimes round their necks under their shirts. They had an illustrious example in the person of George IV, who died with a locket set with a likeness of Mrs Fitzherbert round his neck.

Portrait miniatures were often mounted in the clasps of bracelets. George III's Queen, Charlotte of Mecklenburg-Strelitz (1744-1818), was painted by Sir Thomas Lawrence in 1789 wearing a bracelet set with a miniature of her husband [plate 17].[15] Her granddaughter, Princess Charlotte of Wales, the only child of the Prince Regent, later George IV, died in childbirth in November 1817 and was commemorated by an unusual jewel, probably made to the order of her husband, Prince Leopold of Saxe-Coburg (1790-1865), who was later to become King Leopold I of the Belgians. It is set on the front with the Princess's portrait, probably by the royal miniaturist, Charlotte Jones, surmounted by a crown and on the reverse with her royal arms [plate 16a & b]. The dead Princess's hair, appropriately arranged as the Prince of Wales' feathers, is mounted in an urn-shaped pendent locket, confirming that the jewel was commissioned by someone close to her.

Queen Victoria (who owed her birth to Princess Charlotte's death, which precipitated three of the Regent's younger brothers into matri-

15
Two English gold brooches with silhouette portraits by
John Miers. The sitters are unidentified. One brooch
has a locket fitting
c. 1805
H. 2.5 cms *(left);* 2.4 cms *(right)*
Given by Mr. J. A. Pollak in memory of his mother
M .13 and a-1970

16 a & b
Front and back of an enamelled gold mourning pendant
for Princess Charlotte of Wales (1798-1817); the portrait
miniature by or after the royal miniaturist Charlotte
Jones. Reverse, the Princess's royal arms. The vase-
shaped locket set with hair in front and inscribed on the
reverse *PC 1817*
H. 9.8 cms
Given by Dame Joan Evans, PPSA M.82-1969

17
Oil
Queen Charlotte, consort of
George III, wearing a bracelet set
with a miniature portrait of her
husband
Sir Thomas Lawrence
1789
National Gallery

18 ▶
Watercolour
Queen Victoria
Copy by Lady Abercromby of the
oil painting of 1875 by H. von
Angeli in the Royal Collection
National Portrait Gallery, 708

19

19
Two royal jewels

a
Scarf-pin in gold, the head set with an enamel portrait of Queen Victoria by William Essex (1784-1869) after Winterhalter's painting of 1843 in the Royal Collection
c. 1850
H. 9 cms
Bolckow Bequest 750-1890

b
First Class Badge of the Royal Order of Victoria and Albert. The crown set with diamonds, rubies and emeralds over red enamel above a frame set with brilliant-cut pastes (replacements for diamonds). The double cameo portrait of the Queen and the Prince Consort was engraved in onyx in the Roman workshop of Tommaso Saulini, after the obverse of the Great Exhibition medals by W. Wyon. Signed *T. Saulini.* The setting by R & S Garrard of Panton Street, the Crown Jewellers
c. 1864
H. 8.8 cms
M.180-1976

20
Two English gem-set gold
pendants exemplifying the
language of stones, *c.* 1820–30

a
Heart locket set with a forget-
me-not of turquoises and rubies,
surrounded by a ruby, emerald,
garnet, amethyst, ruby and
diamond, spelling REGARD
H. 3.5 cms
M.20-1983

b
A curving bar with four heart
pendants set with lapis-lazuli,
opal, garnet (used under an old
name, vermeil) and emerald,
spelling LOVE
L. 3.3 cms
M.21-1983

21
Three English seals in gold, about 1815-20

a
Revolving three-sided topaz, one face engraved with the Battle of Trafalgar
(1805) and inscribed *ENGLAND EXPECTS THAT EVERY MAN THIS
DAY WILL DO HIS DUTY*
H. 4.5 cms
Bequeathed by Miss P. M. Sheward M.105-1945

b
Desk seal in the form of an ivory hand clasping a baton with the Gresham
crest at one end and a wolf (from the Gower crest) at the other; the forearm
set with the Leveson-Gower arms
H. 3.3 cms
Given by Mrs. O. C. Leveson-Gower M.8-1972

c
Carnelian intaglio of a female head after Botticelli in a mount enamelled
with forget-me-nots. Bloodstone handle in the form of a parrot
H. 2.3 cms
M.236-1975

mony in the hope of producing an heir to the throne) was a dedicated follower of family tradition. She owned some four bracelets set with portraits of the Prince Consort and, like her grandmother, was painted wearing them [plate 18]. Articles bearing her likeness were among her standard gifts to others [see plate 19a].

The Queen's attitude to sentimental jewellery, however, was unashamedly old-fashioned, though many of her subjects shared her tastes. As early as the second decade of the nineteenth century miniatures, in common with hair, had begun once again to be hidden away in locket fittings inside or at the back of jewellery. This, happily enough for the makers of mass-produced jewellery, left the front of the article concerned free for generalised expressions of sentiment suitable for the needs of most purchasers. In the early years of the nineteenth century the word *Fidelité* (faithfulness) was a popular tag; *GRATITUDE* appears in Gothic characters on the large heart-shaped padlock fastening of a gold chain bracelet of about 1835 in plate 31a. The bracelet is said to have been given by William IV (1765-1837) to his wife, Queen Adelaide (1792-1849), in acknowledgement of her concern for him while he was sick. It is a tribute to his Queen's charity that the bracelet was given to the V&A by a descendant of one of the illegitimate children of William and the actress Mrs Jordan, who were always generously treated by Adelaide.

Padlocks appeared on virtually every type of jewellery in the early nineteenth century. Both Fletcher and Knight illustrated examples, Fletcher's with the motto, *You are the Key,* and Knight's with the alternative, *Thou Hast the Key.* A further variation is furnished by the circular locket in plate 7c; dating to about 1800, it has two pendants, a key and a heart.

A great passion of the early nineteenth century, the language of love in stones, resulted in numerous charming pieces carrying a message or the name of a loved one, exemplified by a heart locket and a charm pendant with hearts in plate 20. The locket, made of coloured gold, is set in the centre with a forget-me-not in turquoises and a ruby, a combination of stones traditionally associated with love.[16] The forget-me-not is a self explanatory example of the language of flowers which enjoyed as great a vogue as that of stones. Surrounding the flower are a ruby, emerald, garnet, amethyst, ruby and diamond, the initial letters of which spell *REGARD.* The pendant is hung with a clutch of jostling hearts set with stones which spell *LOVE* (lapis-lazuli, opal, garnet — used here under an old name — *vermeil*[17] and emerald). Jewellers had occasionally to resort to old terms in order to make up a word. Unhappily their messages have often been ruined subsequently by jewellers who unwittingly replaced missing stones with others which destroyed the word.

In the late eighteenth century and for the first two decades or so of the nineteenth, no gentleman might consider himself well-dressed without a seal or (more often) a bunch of seals dangling from a chain at his waist. These were not merely a fashionable accessory; they were used to seal the letters essential to the conduct of personal, professional or political business. Women also wore seals which were usually suspended on long neckchains. As by no means all wearers were entitled to a coat of arms and crest, engravers like Fletcher and publishers like Knight were ready with suggestions for fancy or punning devices. The jewellers responded by producing inventive new mounts. Of the three examples in plate 21, all dating to between 1810 and 1820, two are for wear and one is a desk seal. An endearing piece made for female use has a hardstone handle in the form of a parrot and is set with a carnelian seal engraved with a female head after Botticelli [plate 21c]; sentiment is added by a forget-me-not on the mount. A desk seal in the shape of a forearm with a carved ivory hand (with its own ring) clutching a baton [plate 21b] was also made for a woman and in this instance her identity is known. At one end of the baton is a grasshopper seal, the crest of the Gresham family, and at the other a wolf, a reference to the Gower crest, while the Leveson-Gower arms are engraved on a seal set in the forearm. Taken together, these point to Catherine Gresham, only daughter and heiress of Sir John Gresham, who married William Leveson-Gower in 1804. The third object [plate 21a] is a revolving three-sided seal of a type usually worn by a man. One facet of the seal depicts the Battle of Trafalgar, fought in October 1805, and is inscribed with Nelson's famous signal, *ENGLAND EXPECTS THAT EVERY MAN THIS DAY WILL DO HIS DUTY*. All the seals cited are engraved on hardstones; cheap versions usually bore fancy devices cast in paste.

Two clasped hands signifying love or friendship, a Roman motif revived in the twelfth century, were among the traditional devices illustrated by Fletcher and Knight. Tiny gold hands, often modelled in the round, singly or together, appeared as fastenings or in place of suspension loops in much jewellery produced in the 1820s and 1830s. Later they were used in such mass-produced pieces as a jet brooch for mourning wear in the form of a hand grasping a branch of yew which dates to about 1875 [plate 22b]. The other mourning jewels in the same illustration [plate 22a & c], a handsome carved jet necklace, and a mass-produced cross in vulcanite or ebonite, represent the black jewellery which no self-respecting female could be without during the Victorian era.

One of the chief European sources of supply of jet lay in the locality of the English town of Whitby, Yorkshire, where jet had been worked from earliest times. The trade had dwindled to near-extinction by the early years of the nineteenth century when it was revived by local enterprise. In ensuing decades, with intermittent hiatuses, the trade expanded to meet what until the 1880s seemed to be an almost inevitable growth of demand. The combination of lathe-turned work with hand-carved details, and the adoption of standardised designs, enabled the leading workshops to turn out large quantities of jet jewellery which was sold in the United Kingdom and exported to countries all over the world. Inevitably imitations of jet were legion.

23▶
Two English mourning buckles in
gold with inscriptions worked in
gold wire over hair, under crystal

a
Inscribed: *Eliz Harman/Obt* 11
Ap/1698 Ata 27
L. 4 cms
M.91-1975

b
Inscribed: *Ann/Harford/1728*
L. 3.4 cms
M.136-1975
Both given by Dame Joan Evans,
PPSA

◀22
Victorian mourning jewellery

a
Jet necklace
c. 1880
L. 48 cms (approx)
Given by Miss B. L. Edmundson
M.65-1974

b
Jet brooch of a hand holding a
spray of yew
*c.*1875
L. 6.2 cms
Anonymous loan

c
Vulcanite cross of roses bound by
ribbon
c. 1875
H. 8.2 cms
Given by Miss A. L. Wyatt
M.17-1971

They included dyed horn, early plastics such as parkesine, a compound of pyroxylin (cellulose nitrate and castor oil),[18] and vulcanite (also known as ebonite), an American invention made from sulphurised rubber.[19] Vulcanite articles are instantly recognizable, for the material eventually turns from black to dark brown on exposure to light, while the underside retains the original colouration. 'French jet' was faceted black glass backed by metal. Perhaps originating in France, it was mainly produced in Bohemia and elsewhere. Other materials used were Irish bog-oak, which from the late 1840s was moulded by steam into intricate interlacing patterns; this was imitated by cheap dyed wood.

The Victorians, like their forebears in the seventeenth century, made much of the ceremonial of death. After the death of George III towards the end of January 1820, his son and successor George IV, who hated mourning, cut short the period of obligatory mourning in unrelieved black to six weeks; the half-mourning which followed in mid-March stipulated black silk and white accessories including white necklaces and earrings for ladies, who were also permitted to wear white or grey clothes on informal occasions. Even this came to an end in April. Unlike George IV, his niece Queen Victoria took a much more dedicated view of mourning requirements, and wore full mourning for each of her uncles for three months instead of the stipulated six weeks[20] The Queen enunciated her views in a letter of 6 June 1858 to her eldest daughter, the Princess Royal, the bride of Prince Frederick William of Prussia. 'Court mournings', Victoria wrote, 'are short and worn here for all Crown Heads and Sovereigns etc. who are no relations — but private mourning we wear as we like; and this private mourning no earthly being can prevent you from wearing in your own home and when you do not appear at Fêtes.' In another letter to her daughter, written on 14 April 1860, the Queen remarked that it was customary in England to wear mourning for close relations such as a brother or sister for six months. The Princess's reply showed that the Prussian practice was much less rigorous, being six weeks for a grandmother and one week for a cousin; two months appeared to be the maximum even for a King.[21]

Immolated in black for the rest of her life after the premature death of her husband on 14 December 1861, Queen Victoria required that everyone at Court wore mourning on social occasions until the end of 1864. Even afterwards, the lady-in-waiting in attendance on the Queen habitually wore black, though the other ladies about her were permitted half-mourning dress. On 10 February 1862, her first wedding anniversary after his death, the Queen instituted the Royal Order of Victoria and Albert in memory of her husband. Membership of the First Class was confined to ladies of royal birth, and the Queen wore her own badge for portraits and on all ceremonial occasions [plate 18]. The First Class Badge in plate 19b dates to about 1864; the fine cameo portrait of Victoria and Albert, engraved after William Wyon's obverse for the Great Exhibition medals, was executed in Rome by Tommaso Saulini, who died in 1864. The original owner, therefore, may have been one of Queen Victoria's elder daughters, but this is no more than conjecture as the piece is undocumented.

The Queen died in 1901, at the height of a new vogue for sentimental jewellery inspired in this instance by a revival of late Georgian design. 'Regard' rings, brooches and pendants were once again high fashion. Lower down the social scale, an eager public existed between the 1870s and the early 1900s for stamped silver jewellery with sentimental messages. This was decorated with the standard devices of love (sometimes expressed in the language of flowers, such as apple-blossom for preference, a china rose for everlasting beauty, a crysanthemum for cheerfulness under adversity, a pansy for 'think of me' and ivy for friendship[22] coupled with popular names such as Ivy, and expressions like *MIZPAH* (a reference to the steadfastness of Ruth: 'ought but death part thee and me').[23] For much of the twentieth century jewellery reverted to a formal character, but as it draws to an end there are signs of a renewed interest in the intricate tokens of affection that so delighted our ancestors.

The Use of Hair in Jewellery

Human hair was used extensively in sentimental jewellery of all kinds; the hair being given by a loved one or removed from the dead before burial. Queen Henrietta Maria (1609-69) seems to have worn a hair bracelet as a token of affection,[24] but bracelets of this type, though certainly often love gifts, were also made as mourning jewellery. In 1647/8 Mary Verney wrote from London to her husband, Sir Ralph (1613-96), who was living in exile in France with their family during the Protectorate, mentioning their young daughter, who had recently died. Lady Verney asked Sir Ralph to send her locks of their daughter's hair 'to make bracelets', adding, 'I know you could not send a more acceptable thing than every one of your sisters a bracelet'.[25]

Men also wore bracelets made from the hair of their loves. The poet and divine John Donne (1571/2-1631) employed his as a potent image of the decay of earthly passions in 'The Relique', where he envisages the excavation of his own grave:

> 'And he that digs it, spies
> A bracelet of bright haire about the bone'.

A Frenchman at the Court of Charles II, who was restored to the throne in 1660, observed some three or four gentlemen sporting bracelets each made from about an ounce of hair bestowed on them by the bold Lady Shrewsbury, one of the more notorious beauties of the day.[26]

Less extravagantly, hair, woven or laid in strands, formed the ground for the motifs used in late-seventeenth and early-eighteenth century slides and lockets, both amatory and commemorative [plates 3 and 24b & c]. Slides were fitted with two flat gold loops at the back through which silk or hair ribbon was threaded for wearing round the neck or the wrist. Tiny, like most lockets of the time, they were commonly put together from standardised components cast or stamped in gold and often enamelled; a few personal details such as initials and inscription were added in gold or gold wire before the whole was protected by a cover of faceted rock crystal. Work of this kind was surprisingly expensive. In 1685 one London woman reported that mourning lockets 'are at least £6 in the making';[27] a costly business, for it was customary for several of these jewels to be ordered for

24
Three late-17th-century English jewels with crystal covers

a
Slide in silver, parcel-gilt, the frame set with blue pastes and pearls, enclosing an enamelled cupid shooting an arrow at a flaming heart on a altar
The reverse enamelled
c. 1690
L. 2.3 cms
M.125-1962

b
Slide in silver, the frame set with pearls, enclosing a gold foil cipher and insignia of Queen Mary II with skull and cross bones mounted over hair and inscribed *Memento Maria Regina obit* 28 *Decembris 1694*
L. 2.9 cms
A & b, given by Dame Joan Evans, PPSA M.107-1962

c
Pendant in gold, the frame set with crystals, enclosing an enamelled cupid with a heart against plaited hair; inscribed *JE ME MEURS MA MERE* (I am dying, Mother) a translation of a line in the 6th-century Greek poet Anacreon's Ode XL
H. 2.9 cms
Frank Ward Bequest M.21-1960

25
Three English jewels with double-sided rock crystal enclosing hair
1746—c. 1800

a
Memorial brooch with silver bow set with rubies and rose — and brilliant-cut diamonds. Pendant locket with enamelled gold ribbon frame, also gem-set, inscribed *Eliz Eyton obit Feb 1754 aet 81*
H. 3.2 cms
M.121-1962

b
Heart-shaped locket with enamelled gold frame, set with emeralds and garnets; inscribed *PRUDENCE FIXES ME OCTR 15 TH.* Reverse engraved *Have my Friendship for Ever Aug 16 1746*
H. 3 cms
M.120-1962

c
Padlock pendant, the frame set with garnets
c. 1800
W. 2.8 cms

a-c, given by Dame Joan Evans, PPSA M.127-1962

distribution among the friends and relatives of the deceased. Many people prudently made financial provision for mourning jewels in their wills, even naming the future recipients.

The hair ground was often overlaid with standard motifs exemplified by the pieces in plate 3. The skeletons in two slides [3a & d] were inspired by the Memento Mori jewels of the Renaissance, which were literally reminders of mortality. Indeed, the upper one, holding a scythe and an hour-glass, the attributes of Time or Death the Reaper, is the personification of Mortality (see also the front endpaper). The jewel commemorates a child who died at the age of three years eight months. The second skeleton, reclining on a tomb chest inscribed *I REST*, is surmounted by two Cupids bearing the initials of the deceased. A skull and cross-bones presides over a more complex emblematic scheme in the third piece [plate 3b]; two Cupids wielding the trumpets of Fame are perched at each end of a tomb inscribed *MEM. MORI*, while between them is a winged hour-glass (or perhaps a heart). Below the tomb are the initials EB, who is recorded in an inscription on the back as having died on 6 February 1697. His (or her) full name is unknown. The slide at the bottom of the group [plate 3c], subsequently converted into a brooch, is simpler: two enamelled gold angels bear a celestial crown over the cipher *AL*. The piece commemorates Sir Andrew Leake, a Naval officer, who was mortally wounded in an attack on Gibraltar in 1704 during the War of the Spanish Succession. Another skull and cross-bones appears on the earlier of the two mourning buckles in plate 23; it commemorates a woman who died in 1698. The second buckle is dated 1728. Both are made of gold, hair and crystal in the manner of the slides and were an adjunct to the mourning clothes conventionally required of the bereaved.

The heavily-faceted crystal fronts of pieces such as these obscured the compositions of gold and hair and made them very private souvenirs. Concealment was often as welcome to lovers as to the grief-stricken bereaved, for the same techniques of construction are used for two amatory jewels in plate 24. Love is naturally represented by Cupid and his traditional accoutrements, described by Donne as

> His sinewy bow, and those immortall darts
> Wherewith he's wont to bruise resisting hearts.[28]

Against a ground of coloured cloth instead of the more usual hair, an enamelled gold Cupid shoots an arrow at a flaming heart upon an altar in one slide [plate 24a]. Another Cupid appears in the locket next to it [plate 24c], mounted over plaited hair and clutching a heart in each hand. He is surrounded by an inscription in gold wire, *JE ME MEURS MA MERE* (I am dying, mother), a cry to Venus from the God of Love.[29]

Evidence of the use of hair in jewellery during the eighteenth century is widespread: hair bracelets, or, in most instances, bracelets set with hair, continued popular. A letter from the Duchess of Port-

26
Plate from an unidentified hairworker's catalogue, *c.* 1840

land to Miss Catherine Collingwood, written on 1st December 1735, strongly suggests that ladies were in the habit of working the hair,[30] leaving the goldsmiths to provide the gold setting. In 1784 Sir William Hamilton the diplomatist, antiquary and collector, gave his niece Mary Hamilton a bracelet containing a lock of his hair which his late wife had worn from the time of her marriage in 1758 until her death in 1782. By his own account, his wife had doted on him and he passed on the bracelet in the consciousness of its importance as a family souvenir.[31]

In mid-century, hair set in transparent double-sided crystal lockets enjoyed considerable popularity as a token of love, affection or mourning. A piece dated 1746 [plate 25b] was clearly made to order. This heart-shaped locket, enclosing the remains of a strand of hair, is set in an enamelled border surmounted by stones and inscribed

27

27

Three late-18th-century English mourning jewels with sepia miniatures

a

Brooch or pin with black-enamelled gold frame; miniature, embellished with carved ivory, gold foil and hair, of a woman seated by a broken column beneath a willow tree, with attendant cherub pointing to the inscription *WEEP NOT IT FALLS TO RISE AGAIN*
c. 1800
H. 3.4 cms
965-1888

b

Locket with black-enamelled gold frame; miniature of a woman seated by a tomb with an urn bearing the initials *IG* and inscribed on the plinth *NOT LOST BUT GONE BEFORE,* while a cherub bears the message *TO BLISS*
About 1790-95
H. 3.9 cms
920-1888

c

Locket with black-enamelled silver-gilt frame set with plaited hair; miniature of a woman standing by a tomb inscribed: *MAY SAINTS EMBRACE THEE WITH A LOVE LIKE MINE*
c. 1790
H. 6.4 cms
937-1888

28

Three English gold mourning jewels, 1791-1818

a

Pendant/brooch set with a white paste cameo of John Wesley on a black ground, inscribed *He rests from his labours.* The reverse engraved *Revd. John Wesley A.M. obt 2 March, 1791 Aet 88*
H. 3.2 cms
Given by Dame Joan Evans, PPSA
M.126-1962

28

b
Chased frame enclosing an
enamelled representation of an
urn and plinth bearing the intials
C : C and the date *1818*. The
reverse engraved *C. Cross ob. 18
March 1818 Aet 48*
L. 2.3 cms
973-1888

c
Pendant; the frame, set with a hair
plait, encloses a wheatsheaf in hair
(the Vasa crest) bound with a
diamond band on blue paste. The
reverse decorated with inscription
in seed pearls *Sir Willliam
Chambers died 8th March 1796 Aged
71*
H. 4.8 cms
M.7-1958

29
Bracelet with a band of twisted
and plaited hair; gold mounts
with applied filigree, set with a
shell cameo possibly representing
Alexander, Roxana and a genius
with torch and arrow
? Swiss in the French manner, *c.*
1825
L. 20.4 cms
Cory Bequest M.64-1951

PRUDENCE ◊ FIXES ◊ ME ◊ OCT^R. ◊ 15TH, and the reverse is engraved *Have My Friendship for Ever Aug 16 1746.* A memorial brooch [plate 25a], a more elaborate version of the amatory piece, is surmounted by a rococo bow with flower sprays in diamonds and rubies. The pendent crystal locket is filled with plaited greying hair, still gummed in place, and set in a scrolling gem-set border, enamelled in black and bearing an inscription recording the death in 1754 of Elizabeth Eyton, aged eighty-one. She was most probably married; the eighteenth-century usage for mourning jewellery was black enamel for a married person, white for an unmarried, although the rule was by no means uniformly observed. A later amatory article, containing a hair curl embellished with gold wire [plate 25c], demonstrates a reversion to closed-back lockets; dating to about 1800, it is in the form of a padlock, much prized in the late eighteenth and early nineteenth centuries as a symbol of captured affection.

The 1760s saw the introduction of a new vogue for mass-produced memorial medallions or lockets which was especially popular in England, though similar work was produced on the Continent.[32] The hair ground in these pieces was replaced by ivory on which were painted compositions in sepia, but tiny snippets of hair were often mixed in with the paint. More easily visible than their late seventeenth century counterparts as the covers of crystal or glass are thin and unfaceted, the execution of these compositions is competent (at best) rather than artistic; the stereotyped repertory of motifs includes obelisks, traditional monuments to fame, columns (sometimes broken for more pathetic effect: see plate 27a), dogs, emblems of fidelity [plates 26 & 27], Cupids in religious guise [plate 27a & b], willows, a sixteenth-century symbol of grief for unrequited love or the loss of a mate [plate 26 & 27a], urns [plate 27c] and females in classical dress [plate 27a & b], who though apparently seated on a convenient bank or rock, perhaps exemplify the biblical prophecy of Isaiah that widows 'being desolate shall sit upon the ground'.[33]

The piece with a broken column [plate 27a], inscribed above *WEEP NOT IT FALLS TO RISE AGAIN,* shows the woman in conventional white classical garb, while the unhappy female in plate 27b, also clothed in a simple dress of classical inspiration, is encouraged by a Cupid bearing a label with the message, *TO BLISS;* further consolation is furnished by the maxim on the plinth of the urn by which she sits, *NOT LOST BUT GONE BEFORE.* The fashionable lady contemplating a funerary urn on a plinth inscribed *MAY SAINTS EMBRACE THEE WITH A LOVE LIKE MINE* in a large pendent medallion is a departure from the general run of designs. The composition is in this instance based on an etching of 1783 by John Raphael Smith (1715-1812), depicting Charlotte at Werther's tomb, after Goethe's enormously popular novel, *Werther* (1774).[34] Nevertheless the inscription on the pendant, though appropriate to the theme of the novel is scarcely less applicable to general needs than the tags on the other pieces, which were carefully selected to suit most customers. The purchasers simply had the name, date of death and age of their loved ones engraved on the back of ready-made articles, though they might occasionally go to the lengths of having the initials of the deceased added to the urn or plinth in the composition, as in plate 27b. This clearly meant that they had to select the miniature on ivory before it was set in its mount.

The rage for these ornaments lasted from the 1770s until after 1800, when the miniaturists were soon ousted by a return to prominence of worked hair devices. Professional hairworkers had always practised their craft, despite the activities of lady amateurs. Women were chiefly employed in the trade, usually under male management, though a few ran their own concerns. Such firms usually reserved part of their output for the great jewellers, who often bought only the hairwork and set it themselves, but in the nineteenth century the hairworkers increasingly undertook both the working and mounting of hair.

In the late eighteenth and early nineteenth centuries a single curl cost under a shilling if plain, but the addition of gold details or the introduction of seed pearls increased the price to five shillings or more, according to the complexity of the design. As the hairworkers prospered, they embarked on ambitious hair compositions, chiefly for mourning jewellery, which were as stereotyped as those of the miniaturists and survived the nineteenth century virtually unchanged. Plate 26, taken from a hairworker's catalogue, shows an early Victorian lady, datable by her curls and the shape of the tomb by which she sits, shadowed by the inevitable willow. As in the seventeenth century, allegedly using the hair provided by their clients, the hairworkers wove and plaited it into bracelets [plate 29] and chains secured with gold fixings, as love tokens. They also made bow brooches, earrings, necklaces and pendants.

The hairworking concerns prospered on mass-production, and, in the Victorian era, by cutting costs to the point at which they attracted a huge popular market, they incurred suspicion that they had long since given up using the hair entrusted to them by their clients. It was so much easier for the trade to obtain hair in bulk from convents on the Continent or other sources of supply that the suspicion was probably justified. Moreover, in their advertisements and catalogues the hairworkers protested too much, each one implying that they were virtually alone in not deceiving the public. In 1872 Alexanna Speight, a London hairworker who naturally claimed to be on the side of the angels, was moved to publish a manual which enabled amateurs to make their own curls and compositions; the sting was in the tail, for Mrs Speight also used the book to advertise her ready-made mounts.[35]

The gum used to fix the hair, and the gold details and half-pearls embellishing the designs, has frequently deteriorated, loosening parts of the composition, even in the most carefully executed pieces. A handsome hair wheatsheaf, heightened with gold wire and bound by a diamond collar, which is mounted on blue paste [plate 28c], has shed a

31
Two gold love tokens

a
Gold ruby bracelet with heart-shaped padlock fastening stamped *GRATITUDE;* gold key
c. 1835
L. 19 cms
Given by Mrs. A. Rolt M.308-1975

b
Gold filigree bracelet with locket fitting in the clasp; set with semi-precious foiled stones and pastes
? English in the French manner,
c. 1825
L. 19 cms
Cory Bequest M.88-1951

Two Victorian mourning jewels in
gold and hair

a
Brooch in gold wire enclosing two
hair curls. The reverse inscribed
*Sir Marc Isambard Brunel died Decr
1849. Aged 80. Sophia Brunel, died
Jany 1855. Aged 79*
L. 4.2 cms
Given by Mrs. A. Kelsey
M.21-1972

b
Bracelet with woven hair; the
gold fixings enamelled in black-
and-white; padlock fastener.
Inscribed *I.S.P. obt Augt 1 1846 aet
33, in memory of J. S. Parker*
L. 21 cms
Given by Mrs. Bertha H. Parker
M.113-1933

32
Three locket pendants, all fitted
with glass-fronted boxes on the
reverse
a
Silver frame with niello decor-
ation enclosing a plaque of
Florentine mosaic representing a
butterfly, a fly and a beetle
Probably German, *c.* 1880
H. 7.4 cms
Given by Mrs. D. R. Bridgeman
M.13-1974

b
Pendant with enamelled gold
frame set with rubies, sapphires
and pearls, enclosing an onyx
cameo portrait of Marie de
Medicis, Queen of France (1573-
1642), after a cameo in the Cabinet
des Médailles, Paris, signed G.
Bissinger. Maker's mark of Carlo
Giuliano
London, *c.* 1865
H. 10.3 cms
165-1900

c
Pendant with cherub terms in
enamelled gold, set with rubies
and hung with pearls
Maker's mark of Carlo Giuliano
London, *c.* 1867
H. 8.7 cms
164-1900
b and c given by Messrs. C. & A.
Giuliano

few of the hairs and one length of gold wire. These have fallen across the plaited hair in the outer frame. The locket, a fine example of the oval pendants or 'medallions' worn by fashionable ladies in the late eighteenth and early nineteenth centuries, commemorates the architect Sir William Chambers (1726-96), who designed Somerset House in 1775.[36]

The rules about the giving and receiving of hair tokens and other sentimental pieces, already in existence in the seventeenth century, were applied with great strictness in the nineteenth century. A young unmarried girl might receive nothing from an unrelated man unless she was betrothed to him, but it was perfectly in order for her to accept such gifts from male and female relatives as well as from female friends. A girl might give an admirer a lock of her hair at his request and accept one in exchange, providing that neither was set in a jewel. These conventions were sometimes disregarded, but never indiscreetly and never without a sense of guilt on the part of a well-bred young girl.

The nineteenth-century passion for hair souvenirs was shared by two English monarchs, George IV (1762-1830) and his niece, Victoria (1819-1901). The Duke of Wellington, who acted as executor to George IV, told the diarist Charles Greville that he had found among the dead king's possessions 'a prodigious quantity of hair — women's hair — of all colours and lengths, some locks with powder and pomatum still sticking to them . . .',[37] souvenirs of the monarch's career as a womaniser, begun in adolescence. As Prince of Wales, one of his earliest loves was Sir William Hamilton's niece, Mary, in 1779 a young woman of twenty-three employed in the Royal Household. The Prince was only seventeen, and for the rest of his life he was to prefer women older than he. The Prince begged Miss Hamilton to give him a piece of jewellery set with a lock of her hair and inscribed with her name, date of birth and the motto, *Toujours aimée* (loved for ever), an ironical request viewed in retrospect. In return he asked her permission to present her with a bracelet set with his hair and inscribed either with the same sentiment or with another, *Tout ce qui m'est chère au monde* (All that is dear to me in the world.)[38] Mary Hamilton was too prudent to encourage him, but the encounter serves to show that the language of love in England was often French, as it was elsewhere in Europe. Hence jewellery bearing French inscriptions cannot automatically be ascribed to France.

Queen Victoria both wore and gave jewellery set with hair, a practice inculcated in her earliest days by her mother. From the time of her engagement to Prince Albert of Saxe-Coburg-Gotha late in 1839 the Queen was never without a lock of her beloved's hair on her person. She put it in lockets, brooches, bracelets and other items of jewellery. After Albert's premature death in December 1861 the Queen clung ever more tenaciously to the relics of her husband.

The Queen also scattered her own hair among her family, and bestowed it on others as a mark of special favour. Among the latter was the Empress Eugénie of France (1826-1920), who came with her husband Napoleon III on a state visit to England in 1855. Victoria took to the Empress immediately, and noted with satisfaction in her Journal on 20 April 1855 that Eugénie 'was touched to tears when I gave her a bracelet with my hair'.[39]

The general unadventurous nature of the hair trade downgraded it in the course of the nineteenth century. At first hairwork was associated with fashionable designs, as in the bracelet in plate 29, a love token dating to about 1825. The hair band is secured in gold mounts elaborately decorated with filigree in the current late Neoclassical manner, while the clasp is set with a shell cameo. Another bracelet, also of hair and gold [plate 30b], inscribed in memory of J.S.Parker and dated 1846, again follows the form of fashionable jewellery of the time. But the twin hair curls mounted in a brooch of looped gold wire of about 1855 in plate 30a, commemorating the father of the great engineer, Sir Marc Isambard Brunel (1769-1849) and his wife Sophia, who outlived him by six years, are manifestly of the same type as that set in the garnet padlock of about 1800 in plate 25c. From 1850 hair curls increasingly appeared in cheap mass-produced mounts in gilt and plated metal, without claim to fashion.

Even in the early years of the nineteenth century, when hair bracelets were frequently worn, there were signs that some women at least preferred to keep their hair souvenirs out of sight in locket fittings secreted in the back of jewellery. Known as 'boxes' in the nineteenth century, these fittings were widespread. There is one in the clasp of the bracelet in plate 31b, which was made in about 1830. The front of the piece, busy with applied filigree and coloured stones, gives no indication of the locket behind. The three pendants in plate 32, all variations of the lockets worn by everyone with any pretensions to smartness between about 1860 and 1885, are fitted with boxes which are now empty. The depth of the fittings, however, indicates that they were intended for hair and not for photographs, which had already succeeded in making painted miniatures obsolescent if not obsolete. Hair must likewise have gone into some of the locket pendants on the black-enamelled gold bracelet in plate 33a which, with a brooch [plate 33c], both dating to the 1860s, were designed for use in the later stages of mourning after the initial period of unrelieved immolation in black had passed. Both pieces are set with diamonds and pearls which, being regarded as uncoloured, were acceptable as adjuncts to the greys and lilacs often worn as half-mourning. The brooch and bracelet are in the so-called Moroccan style, the speciality of a Parisian jeweller named Crouzet (c.1816-c.95), but they may be English copies of his work. The diamond-set devices on the bracelet include an anchor (Hope), a cross (Faith), a heart, a star (presumably an allusion to the star that guided the Three Kings), and the initial A, perhaps that of the person commemorated. An oval locket bearing a Gothic initial L executed in diamonds and black enamel [plate 33b] has retained both its photograph and hair; the back is inscribed: *In remembrance of L.B.F. Oct 7th 1871, from C.G.S.F.*

33
Victorian mourning jewellery, all black-enamelled gold

a
Bracelet and locket pendants set with pearls and brilliant-cut diamonds; the pendants decorated with the letter A, a cross (Faith), an anchor (Hope), a heart (Love) and a star. Perhaps inspired by work in the Moroccan manner by Crouzet senior of Paris.
? English, c. 1860
Diam. (closed) 7.7 cms
M.104-1951

b
Locket with letter L in brilliant-cut diamonds and enamel; a commemorative inscription on the reverse dated October 7, 1871. Inside, hair and a photograph of a young woman wearing a locket
English, 1871/2
H. 6 cms
Given by Mrs. O. C. Leveson-Gower M.11-1972

c
Brooch with pendants, set with pearls, rose- and brilliant-cut diamonds. In the manner of Crouzet
English, c. 1865
H. 7.6 cms
M.120-1951
a and c Cory Bequest

Notes

1 W. Congreve, *Love for Love: a Comedy*, 1695, Act 3, Scene 1.

2 S. Bury, *Rings*, HMSO, 1984.

3 M. Corbett and R. W. Lightbown, *The Comely Frontispiece*, London, 1969, p.11.

4 Petrarch (Francesco Petrarca, 1304-74), Italian poet, humanist, scholar and diplomat.

5 Artists of the Tudor Court, the portrait miniature rediscovered, 1520-1620; catalogue of an exhibition of the V&A, July-November 1983, by Sir Roy Strong with contributions by V. J. Murrell, cat. no.163. An analogy with the phoenix is also suggested.

6 Otto van Veen (1558-1629), studied and worked in the Low Countries and Italy; settled at Antwerp in 1593, publishing several emblem books between 1607 and 1618. *Amorvm Emblemata* was dedicated to William Herbert, Earl of Pembroke and his brother.

7 'Renewned Carlos! Thow has won the day
(Loyalty Lost) by helpin Charles away,
From Kings-Blood-Thirsty-Rebels in a Night,
made black with Rage, of thieves, & Hells dispight (etc.)

8 J. Evans, *A History of Jewellery*, 2 ed., 1970, p.144.

9 Mrs. Masham was a cousin of the Duchess of Marlborough.

10 Corbett and Lightbown, op.cit., p.11.

11 Genesis, 8, 8-11.

12 Shakespeare, *As You Like It*, Act 2, scene 7.

13 G. C. Williamson, 'Miniature Paintings of Eyes', *Connoisseur*, 10, 1904, pp.147-149.

14 W. H. Wilkins, *Mrs. Fitzherbert and George IV*, 2 vols, 1905, II, pp.219-223. Wilkins in effect contradicts Williamson's claim that the eye was Mrs. Fitzherbert's; moreover Williamson states that the miniaturist George Engleheart painted an eye in 1796.

15 Queen Charlotte gave Lawrence only one sitting; her dresser, Mrs. Papendiek, had afterwards to pose wearing the jewellery.

16 I am indebted to Charlotte Gere for this information.

17 According to Geoffrey Munn, the definition appears in Webster's *Dictionary*.

18 The inventor was Alexander Parkes (1830-90), chemist; his plastic was the subject of several patents from 1855 onwards. It was also known as xylonite and was the precurser of celluloid.

19 The American Charles Goodyear (1800-60) was the first to patent (in 1844) the process of stabilizing rubber by combining it with sulphur.

20 R. Fulford, ed., Dearest Child, *Letters between Queen Victoria and the Princes Royal*, 1858-61, 1964, p.247.

21 Id., pp.110, 247.

22 See Rev. Robert Tyas, *The Sentiment of Flowers*, Edinburgh, c. 1835.

23 Ruth, 1, 17.

24 Kings and Queens exhibition, The Queen's Gallery, Buckingham Palace, 1982-83, cat. no.31. Oliver Millar, *Van Dyck in England*, National Portrait Gallery, London, 1982-83, cat. no.8.

25 *Memoirs of the Verney Family*, compiled by F. P. Verney, 2 vols., 1892, II, p.316.

26 Count de Grammont, *Memoirs*, quoted in E.S.Turner, *The Court of St James's*, 1959, p. 161.

27 C.Aspinall-Oglander, *Nunwell Symphony*, 1945, p.148.

28 John Donne, Elegy XVII ('Variety').

29 The use of a French quotation (probably a translation from the Greek by Mathurin Regniers) is perhaps another instance of the international use of French as the language of love.

30 Lady Llanover, ed., *The Autobiography and Correspondence of Mary Granville, Mrs. Delany*, 1st series, 3 vols, 1861, I, P.543.

31 E. & F. Anson, eds., *Mary Hamilton, afterwards Mrs. John Dickenson, at Court and at Home. From Letters and Diaries, 1756-1816*, 1925, p.159.

32 G.Zick, *Gedenke mein, Freundschafts- und Memorialschmuck, 1770-1870*, Dortmund, 1980, pl.20, 22, passim.

33 Isaiah, 3, 26.

34 Zick, op.cit., pp.155-6. Another variation of Smith's composition is in the V&A (942-1888).

35 A.Speight, *The Lock of Hair*, 1872.

36 The locket was transferred to the V&A by the National Portrait Gallery from a bequest of relics of Sir William Chambers.

37 H.Reeve (ed.), *The Greville Memoirs*. vols, 5 ed., 1875, II, pp.189-190, 8 September 1831.

38 Anson, op.cit, pp.74-75.

39 RA Queen Victoria's Journal.

Further Reading

There is a paucity of books on sentimental jewellery, though some pieces are illustrated in general studies such as Joan Evans, *A History of Jewellery*, cited in the footnotes, and in catalogues such as *Princely Magnificence, Court Jewels of the Renaissance, 1500-1630*, an exhibition mounted by Anna Somers Cocks at the V&A in 1980.
Mario Praz, *Studies in Seventeenth-Century Imagery*, 2 ed., Rome, 1964, furnishes a bibliography of emblem books.
Helen Muller, *Jet Jewellery and Ornaments*, Shire Publications Ltd, 1980, and Diana Cooper and Norman Battershill, *Victorian Sentimental Jewellery*, David & Charles, Newton Abbot, 1972, are the only specialist publications of recent years.
Mourning jewellery is illustrated and discussed in John Morley, *Death, Heaven and the Victorians*, 1971, and Lou Taylor, *Mourning Dress*, 1983.

BACK ENDPAPER *(left)*
Designs for jewellery
Hand-coloured etching; plate 7 from Pouget fils
Traité des Pierres Précieuses, Paris, 1762
V & A Library

BACK ENDPAPER *(right)*
Designs for girandole earrings
Hand-coloured etching; plate 13 from Pouget fils,
Traité des Pierres Précieuses, Paris, 1762
V & A Library